© Dante Chiarre

LIMITING INTERFERENCE IN LIFE

DANTE A. CHIARRE

"Notice what you defend."

PUBLISHED BY
Chiarre Press

ISBN: 979-8-9944230-0-4
Copyright © 2026 Dante A. Chiarre
All rights reserved.

Acknowledgments

This book was shaped through experience and dialogue.
Many thanks to the few who listened closely,
challenged what was unclear,
and helped keep the signal simple.

CONTENTS

MOVEMENT I — System Behavior

   Systems Settle When Pressure Is Removed
   Why Forcing Understanding Slows Understanding
   Stability Is a Physical State Before It Is a Mental One

MOVEMENT II — Sources of Interference

   Attention Precedes Meaning
   Effort Applied to the Wrong Layer
   Identity Amplifies Distortion
   Why Explanation Degrades Integration
   When Improvement Becomes Noise

MOVEMENT III — Orientation & Timing

   Facing Events Without Absorbing Them
   Waiting Is an Active Condition
   The Difference Between Motion and Direction
   Behavior Has Gravity

MOVEMENT IV — Resolution

   Less Is More
   Coherence Attracts Without Intention
   Order Appears When Resistance Stops
   Why Chasing Outcomes Repels Them
   Non-Interference Is Not Inaction
   Why Most Practices Eventually Fail
   What Remains When Noise Stops
   Nothing Further Is Required

MOVEMENT I
SYSTEM BEHAVIOR

SYSTEMS SETTLE WHEN PRESSURE IS REMOVED

Most systems do not need improvement.
They need relief.

When pressure is applied to a system that is already adjusting, the adaptation slows.
When pressure is removed, correction resumes on its own.

This is observable everywhere.
In bodies.
In conversations.
In decisions.

The mistake is assuming that visible effort is required for progress.
Often, effort is the interruption.

WHY FORCING UNDERSTANDING SLOWS UNDERSTANDING

Understanding has its own timing.

When meaning is pursued too early, it hardens.
What might have remained flexible becomes fixed.
What could have integrated naturally becomes an idea to defend.

This is why clarity often arrives after attention relaxes.
Not before.

Understanding follows stability.
It does not precede it.

STABILITY IS A PHYSICAL STATE BEFORE IT IS A MENTAL ONE

Mental clarity is downstream.

Before thoughts align, the system must settle.
Before interpretation becomes accurate, orientation must stabilize.

Attempts to define meaning during instability produce convincing errors.
They feel urgent.
They feel important.
They feel right.

They are usually noise.

MOVEMENT II
SOURCES OF INTERFERENCE

ATTENTION PRECEDES MEANING

Nothing acquires meaning until attention lands.

Meaning does not exist independently.
It forms in response to where attention focuses and how tightly it grips.

When attention is scattered, meaning fragments.
When attention is fixed, meaning narrows.
When attention is consistent, meaning clarifies without effort.

EFFORT APPLIED
TO THE WRONG LAYER

Most effort fails because it is applied to the surface.

People try to correct conclusions instead of orientation.
They adjust outcomes instead of conditions.
They refine explanations instead of attention.

This creates movement without direction.

Effort becomes productive only when it touches the correct layer.
Often, that layer requires less effort, not more.

IDENTITY AMPLIFIES DISTORTION

Identity magnifies whatever passes through it.

A thought becomes personal.
An event becomes defining.
A reaction becomes a position.

Without identity, events pass cleanly.
With identity, they accumulate.

This accumulation is mistaken for experience.
It is actually residual distortion.

WHY EXPLANATION DEGRADES INTEGRATION

Explanation freezes what is still moving.

When something is explained too soon, its movement stops. What was integrating becomes an object.

This is why silence often completes processes that speech interrupts.

Not because silence is superior,
but because it allows continuity.

WHEN IMPROVEMENT BECOMES NOISE

Improvement is useful until it becomes habitual.

Once improvement continues without necessity, it creates interference.

Refinement replaces responsiveness.
Adjustment replaces awareness.

At that point, improvement no longer improves.
It destabilizes.

MOVEMENT III
ORIENTATION & TIMING

FACING EVENTS WITHOUT ABSORBING THEM

Events do not require absorption to be experienced.

They require contact, not capture.

When events are absorbed, they become internal weather.
When they are observed, they pass through.

The difference is subtle.
The consequences are not.

WAITING IS AN ACTIVE CONDITION

Waiting is not the absence of action.
It is the presence of restraint.

In waiting, orientation remains intact.
In premature action, orientation fractures.

Waiting preserves optionality.
Action ceases it.

THE DIFFERENCE BETWEEN MOTION AND DIRECTION

Motion feels productive.
Direction feels quiet.

Motion responds to pressure.
Direction responds to alignment.

A system can move rapidly and go nowhere.
Or it can move slowly and arrive.

Urgency is not a signal.
Orientation is.

BEHAVIOR HAS GRAVITY

Behavior repeats what it reinforces.

Not because of belief.
Not because of intention.
But because repetition stabilizes patterns.

What is enacted consistently gains momentum.
What is resisted inconsistently persists.

This is involuntary.

MOVEMENT IV
RESOLUTION

LESS IS MORE

Most systems fail from excess, not lack.

Additional inputs complicate signals.
Additional strategies dilute coherence.

When unnecessary elements are removed,
what remains organizes itself.

This appears effortless only because the effort was never required.

COHERENCE ATTRACTS WITHOUT INTENTION

When a system is coherent, it becomes predictable.
Predictability invites alignment.

Others respond not to effort,
but to consistency.

Attraction is a side effect of order.
It does not need to be pursued.

ORDER APPEARS
WHEN RESISTANCE STOPS

Resistance fragments attention.

When resistance drops, attention unifies.
When attention unifies, order appears.

This is often mistaken for success.
It is simply the absence of interference.

WHY CHASING OUTCOMES REPELS THEM

Outcomes pursued directly distort behavior.

Behavior bends toward the result instead of the condition.
This introduces tension.

Tension destabilizes coherence.
Coherence is what outcomes follow.

The pursuit undermines the mechanism.

NON-INTERFERENCE IS NOT INACTION

Non-interference is selective restraint.

It requires discernment.
It requires timing.

Doing nothing indiscriminately is neglect.
Intervening indiscriminately is disruption.

WHY MOST PRACTICES EVENTUALLY FAIL

Practices fail when they outlive their function.

What once stabilized becomes ritual.
What once clarified becomes repetition.

When a practice is continued for its own sake,
it replaces responsiveness.

Responsiveness cannot be practiced.
It can only be allowed.

WHAT REMAINS WHEN NOISE STOPS

When noise subsides, nothing new appears.

What remains was already present.

It was simply obscured by activity.

NOTHING FURTHER IS REQUIRED

At some point, addition becomes avoidance.

When orientation is stable,
there is nothing to improve,
nothing to resolve,
nothing to pursue.

The system continues on its own.

Interference is optional.

About the Author

Dante Chiarre is a private author.
These texts come from lived practice and careful observation, shaped over time into a form that can be carried, shared, and returned to.

Made in the USA
Coppell, TX
20 January 2026

69688321R00023